COMMUNITY WORKERS

A Librarian's Job

VIRGINIA O'BRIAN

Cavendish
Square
New York

Published in 2015 by Cavendish Square Publishing, LLC
243 5th Avenue, Suite 136, New York, NY 10016

Copyright © 2015 by Cavendish Square Publishing, LLC

First Edition

Website: cavendishsq.com

This publication represents the opinions and views of the author based on his or her personal experience, knowledge, and research. The information in this book serves as a general guide only. The author and publisher have used their best efforts in preparing this book and disclaim liability rising directly or indirectly from the use and application of this book.

CPSIA Compliance Information: Batch #WS14CSQ

All websites were available and accurate when this book was sent to press.

Library of Congress Cataloging-in-Publication Data
O'Brian, Virginia.
A librarian's job / by Virginia O'Brian.
p. cm. — (Community workers)
Includes index.
ISBN 978-1-62712-357-0 (hardcover) ISBN 978-1-62712-358-7 (paperback) ISBN 978-1-62712-360-0 (ebook)
1. Librarians — Juvenile literature. 2. Libraries — Juvenile literature. I. Title.

Z682.O27 2015
020.23—d23

Editorial Director: Dean Miller
Editor: Amy Hayes
Senior Copy Editor: Wendy A. Reynolds
Art Director: Jeffrey Talbot
Designer: Douglas Brooks
Photo Researcher: J8 Media
Production Manager: Jennifer Ryder-Talbot
Production Editor: David McNamara

The photographs in this book are used by permission and through the courtesy of: Cover photo by kali9/E+/Getty Images; Tyler Olson/Shutterstock.com, 5; Robert Kneschke/Shutterstock.com, 7; Jupiterimages/Stockbyte/Getty Images, 9; kali9/E+/Getty Images, 11; Lisa F. Young/Shutterstock.com, 13; Bildagentur Waldhaeus, 15; Steve Debenport/E+/Getty Images, 17; andresrimaging/iStock/Thinkstock, 19; Kali Nine LLC/E+/Getty Images, 21.

Printed in the United States of America

Contents

Librarians like to help people.

Librarians help people find things in the **library**.

I help people find what
they need in the library.

I help people find the answers
to their questions.

This person wants a certain **magazine**.

I show her how to find it in the **catalog**.

The catalog is a list of everything in the library.

Andre is doing a report
for school.

He needs to find the right book.

I show him where to look.

Addison is having trouble with the computer.

I help her use it.

I answer questions in the **digital media** section.

I help people find **audiobooks**, CDs, and DVDs.

15

I check books out to people.

I print out a **receipt**.

The receipt tells people when the books are **due**.

Every day, books are **returned** to the library.

I put each book back on the bookshelf.

A librarian has a busy job.

I am never too busy to answer a question.

I am always here to help.

Words to Know

audiobooks (**aw**-dee-oh-buhkz) tapes or CDs of people reading books aloud

catalog (**ka**-tuh-log) a list of all the books and materials in the library, often on a computer

digital media (**di**-ji-tul **mee**-dee-ya) materials that are used with an electronic device including audiobooks, CDs, and DVDs

due (**doo**) books or other materials that need to be brought back to the library

librarian (ly-**brer**-ee-en) a person who works at a library

library (**ly**-brer-ee) a building where materials such as books and videos can be borrowed

magazine (**ma**-geh-zeen) a kind of book that has news, stories, and pictures

receipt (ree-**seet**) a paper that tells you when books are due

returned (ree-**turnd**) given back

22

Find Out More

Books

Check It Out! Reading, Finding, Helping
by Patricia Hubbell, Marshall Cavendish

I Want to Be a Librarian
by Dan Liebman, Firefly Books

The Librarian From the Black Lagoon
by Mike Thaler, Spotlight Publications

Website

At Your Library
www.atyourlibrary.org/whats-library

Index